This book belongs to

. . . .

The Art of
KINDNESS

Meredith Gaston

Hardie Grant

BOOKS

TABLE OF CONTENTS

DEAREST YOU,

There could be no greater time than now to deeply understand and practise the art of kindness in daily life. In this busy, bustling and impatient world we call home, a world that too often seems brash, disconnected and overwhelming, kindness remains a breath of fresh air. A life-affirming anchor. An uncomplicated, healing source of comfort and joy.

To me, kindness is higher love in action. I see higher love as an open, all-encompassing love that doesn't ask for anything in particular in return: a non-judgemental, respectful and inclusive love. Such love encompasses a broader, more expansive yearning to see ourselves, others and our earth acknowledged, loved and supported. It seems to me that a deficit of kindness is a missing link we all too often sense.

Kindness is universally understood. It is shared and felt through our intentions, thoughts, speech, actions, gestures, touch and gaze. Indeed, we can be kind with our hands, our words and our eyes: with a sincere compliment, a true smile, a helping hand, an expression of comfort or a random act of giving. And while kindness is free to give, the richness it brings to ourselves and others is beyond measure. Moreover, when it comes to challenges, disagreements or struggles of any kind, there is nothing as disarming or healing as kindness.

Kindness is transformative and its effects cannot be underestimated. A single act of kindness has the power to change someone's day; in some cases, it can turn a life around. This is because kindness is not only seen or known: it is felt in the heart. As poet and author Maya Angelou taught, people will likely forget your precise words and actions, but they will never forget how you made them feel. Mother Teresa suggested that we be kind whenever possible, reminding us in the same breath that it is *always* possible.

How profound it is to see kindness as an option we possess in every moment; to see that each day, we have the power to make a positive difference in our own lives and the lives of others. Indeed, every thought, every action, every person, every moment, every feeling and every belief can be transformed by kindness. We too often undervalue our ability to bring peace and joy to others and to ourselves. We forget how gently we can change the world.

The sense of elevation we experience through practising kindness provides us with a sustainable sense of contentment, along with a zest for life. This is because kindness cannot help but create and spread new, positive energy. Unkind thoughts and actions deplete us as they inevitably lead to negativity, disappointment and exhaustion. Kind thoughts and actions facilitate meaningful connections of all sorts, and strengthen us, body, mind and spirit. The biology of kindness is such that natural, feel-good chemicals are distributed throughout our bodies when we give and receive kindness. In other words, kindness literally does good on a cellular level, supporting and expanding our sense of wellbeing in daily life. Giving and receiving kindness nourishes, energises and uplifts us so that we may not only live our own dreams; we may encourage others to do the same.

This book is intended to help you foster kindness in your life. It is in three parts: Kindness and Self-care, Connective Kindness, and Kindness Towards Our Earth.

Chapter one

KINDNESS AND SELF-CARE

Kindness begins with us. When we are kind to ourselves, we fulfil, honour and nourish ourselves. We may be in the habit of berating and criticising ourselves for our perceived shortcomings, constantly second-guessing ourselves, putting our own needs last or disallowing ourselves the time, space and patience we deeply need to rest, heal and feel content. We may be our own harshest critics, finding it second nature to criticise ourselves yet very challenging to praise and comfort ourselves.

Alas, we cannot pour from empty cups. In this chapter we will explore how caring for and loving ourselves with patience and kindness fortifies us for life, while positively transforming our world and experiences. Quite simply, when we look after ourselves with patient and unconditional kindness, we flourish.

Seeing ourselves through kinder eyes makes a world of difference, and it is something each and every one of us can learn to do. We can each build solid inner foundations through kindness, strengthening ourselves with our own love, comfort and joy.

In my eyes, kindness towards ourselves is the highest success we can achieve in this life. Through practising the joyous art of kindnesss in daily life, we may finally see and experience ourselves as the fulsome, loving and capable human beings that we are.

Chapter two

CONNECTIVE KINDNESS

In being kinder to ourselves, we cannot help but become kinder to others too. When we think, speak and act in kindness towards others, we strengthen our collective wellbeing, enhance our relationships and enrich our lives.

Real kindness does not ask for anything in return; it is unto itself whole and complete. Kindness with an agenda is a form of transaction, rather than higher love in action. True kindness in relationships is about honouring one another, and possessing a genuine desire to see each other happy, healthy and fulfilled.

In this chapter you will find inspiration to cultivate kindness in all your relationships and explore the magical, connective and life-changing powers of kindness in daily life.

Chapter three

KINDNESS TOWARDS OUR EARTH

Our Mother Earth is a magnificent being who requires our kindness more than ever before. We are starting to hear her stronger call for kindness now, as the immensity of the toll we have taken upon her becomes uncomfortably visible.

Practising kindness towards our earth and all her creatures involves treading lightly, acknowledging her mystery and splendour, and seeing ourselves as part of, not separate from or superior to, nature.

In this final chapter we will explore the ways in which kindness extends well beyond ourselves, our own life experiences and self-importance – even beyond our own space and time. We will look at the idea of planting trees under whose shade we may never sit, choosing kindness as nourishment for our present and future earth, and for all those who will come after us.

If all things are connected in this life, and I believe that they are, then kindness to one is kindness to all. With more kindness in circulation, we will see our world soften and open. Priorities will realign to meet our deepest values as human beings, and we will begin to grow and experience peace at last. The questions or stresses that we face, both personally and collectively, may be complicated, but the answers will always be simple.

Even in the face of unkindness, we are called to be kind. While it may sometimes take time and a change in perspective to see the deep-running benefits of the higher roads we take in life, we do well to take them every time. Unkindness often stems from hurt, and hurt upon hurt creates fear, pain and further disconnection. What remains a constant is the common thread that ties us all together: our need for connection; our need for love. We all need to feel that we belong, that we are of value; that we are seen, heard, safe and understood.

Let kindness begin with us, and let us change the world.

Meredith ♥ X

ENJOYING THIS BOOK

As you turn the pages of this book, we will dip deeply into kindness together. There will be spaces for rest and spaces for play; spaces for reflection and spaces for action. Your words and memories, hopes and dreams are all welcomed within.

This book is arranged in three sections: Kindness and Self-care, Connective Kindness, and Kindness Towards Our Earth. You may wish to read these in order, or dip in and out of different sections according to your mood or interests. You may wish to do the exercises more than once, tracing your changing responses over time.

One extremely effective way I have found to practise the meditations and positive affirmations within this book is to record my own voice reading the steps out loud, then play it back, guiding me through the whole process. There is a deep sense of trust established when we hear our own voice, and it is a powerful, simple way to move through these meditations in your own space and at your own pace.

This is your book and your time. Please enjoy it.

KINDNESS AND SELF-CARE

KINDNESS AS SELF-CARE

Being kind towards ourselves is not necessarily something we were taught how to do. We may have been taught manners or etiquette, both kindnesses of sorts, or we may have witnessed kindness in action in our homes and communities. Yet understanding the role that kindness plays in cultivating our wellness and self-worth is an essential aspect of our emotional intelligence, well deserving of our time, care and attention.

When we are kind to ourselves we see ourselves as worthy of our own tenderness. We acknowledge that we are naturally deserving of fulfilment and peace, and we grant ourselves permission to seek and savour goodnesses of all kinds in daily life. When we think kindly about ourselves, we nurture and grow our self-esteem and confidence. We learn to soothe and comfort ourselves through all the seasons of our lives, quelling any restless or fearful feelings we may meet with our very own gentle, loving and ever-available care.

Through kindness we come to know an uplifted state of being in which we readily see the positives in ourselves, our lives and others with greater ease. Practising kindness towards ourselves as well as others, we strengthen inner feelings of belonging, comfort and contentment. Once we find comfort and belonging within ourselves, we find the world around us naturally echoing our joy.

We may have become unkind to ourselves over time. There may be parts of ourselves that we do not like, for whatever reason. Perhaps we see ourselves

through others' eyes rather than our own. Perhaps we simply forget how unique and valuable we are, or neglect to be grateful for ourselves and our lives. Yet there is no hurt, no lost or berated part of ourselves that cannot be touched by our own loving kindness. Indeed, little kindnesses towards ourselves made habitual in daily life are enough to turn any tide, bit by bit, day by day. We can be what we are looking for, and gently but surely learn to love ourselves in the way we yearn to know. In my eyes, self-care *is* self-love.

It is never too late to be kind and loving towards ourselves. In fact, the best time is now. The past has gone and the future is not yet here. We needn't wait until we change to love ourselves; we can love ourselves just as we are right now. We can choose to treat ourselves with the kindness we deserve, and move gently, confidently forward in the direction of our dreams.

EVERYTHING IN
THE UNIVERSE
IS WITHIN YOU.
ASK ALL FROM
YOURSELF.

Rumi

KINDNESS AND GOOD ENERGY

Self-care shapes our personal energy, the energy with which we introduce ourselves before we even speak. When we are kind to ourselves and look after ourselves lovingly, we exude a sense of grace and self-worth, setting the tone for all other relationships we will ever experience.

In other words, when we are kind to ourselves, it is natural that others will sense it and follow suit. The people with whom we share our world play major roles in shaping our health and happiness too, so this connective aspect of kindness and our personal energy is very important for us to acknowledge.

As French writer Pierre Corneille said, 'Self-love is the source of all our other loves.' With a baseline of kindness towards ourselves, it is much easier to be kind towards others. This is because we possess a better frame of mind, feel more relaxed, more comfortable and energised, and, in being fulfilled ourselves, are better able to nourish others. Through our commitment to kindness we simply feel better, do better and blossom more beautifully as human beings.

When we are kind, people are drawn to the comfort, joy and inspiration we possess and share. We are never short of friendship, peace and love when our energy is open and kind. Indeed, kindness is magnetic, beautiful and beautifying. It allows us to sparkle from the inside out, drawing all the more fullness and joy into our inner worlds, and into the world around us.

KINDNESS AND WELLNESS

The thoughts we think and the feelings we feel are vibrational. They permeate not only our minds but our entire bodies. It is life-changing to realise that our daily attitudes and behavioural choices directly shape our wellbeing at a cellular level. Indeed, positive mindfulness practices such as gratitude and kindness are proven to support, enhance, even radically transform, our physical health.

Giving and receiving kindness is rather magical. Kindness feels light and energising but is all at once truly grounding for our minds and bodies. Kindness releases serotonin and oxytocin throughout our body systems, activating our natural feel-good resources. Kindness fortifies, beautifies, soothes and uplifts us. Recent studies have shown that kindness even contributes to graceful ageing and the health of our hearts. It is no surprise that the happiest people are giving people: people who help themselves and others to change their lives. As Saint Francis of Assisi so wonderfully taught, it is in giving that we receive.

When we practise kindness as self-care, we begin to sense greater relaxation, resilience and fulfilment within ourselves. Over time as we come to know a kinder inner voice and see ourselves through kinder eyes, we experience the self-respect and self-worth we deserve to know. As a wonderful side-effect, cultivating self-kindness helps us to find and grow healthy, nourishing relationships in the outer world with others: bonds that support our wellness to blossom all the more.

Through higher love towards ourselves – love that doesn't judge, that is gentle, patient and forgiving – we cultivate inner peace, courage and vitality. We learn to comfort and care for ourselves unconditionally, no matter what life may bring.

FOR IT IS IN GIVING THAT WE RECEIVE.

Francis of Assisi

MAY YOUR
INNER VOICE
BE THE
KINDEST VOICE
YOU KNOW.

m

KINDER THOUGHTS, KINDER SELF-TALK

Kindness towards ourselves begins with our thoughts. The thoughts we choose to think determine our self-talk, words, actions and personal experiences. Unkind thoughts and actions create tension, anxiety and disconnection, while kind thoughts grow the delicious feelings of peace, balance and connection we seek.

The nature and quality of the thoughts we choose to think determine our self-talk. Our self-talk is the internal monologue we experience moment to moment, the inner voice telling us how good or bad we are, how right or wrong we are, or how worthy or unworthy we may be. It is the voice we hear more than any other voice in our lives, that critiques and monitors us, that approves and disapproves of us, and that actively shapes our life and our world. This inner voice is usually far more critical and unkind than a close friend or family member would ever be. Indeed, if this voice belonged to somebody we knew, we would likely choose never to see them again!

Yet we are with ourselves for life. Our relationship with ourselves is the most precious, long-term and significant one we will ever know. We cannot continue to suffer our own unkindness. Our inner voice must be the one to comfort and inspire us, motivate and soothe us, love and nurture us. Our inner voice is our greatest asset, and it must be the kindest voice we know.

GROW LOVELY
THOUGHTS
AND LET THEM
DELIGHT YOU.

m

FINDING A KINDER INNER VOICE

It is important to realise that our inner voice is something we can reprogram. Our inner voice is part subconscious, part conscious mind, and more often than not is composed of old, outworn voices, possibly those of our parents or other significant figures, voices we accidentally adopted somewhere along our path and now consider as our own.

However, thoughts are by nature ever changing, creative and flexible. They are habit patterns open to transformation. Just because we have thought a certain way for a long time does not mean that such thinking is our permanent setting. That we have been unkind to ourselves for a long time does not prohibit us from being kind to ourselves right now, and from now on.

While we may never have framed our habitual thinking in such a way, being self-critical and self-deprecating, second-guessing ourselves and overindulging in regretful retrospection are all unkindnesses towards ourselves. When we are kinder to ourselves, we develop greater self-assuredness. We question ourselves less, praise and comfort ourselves more. Kinder thoughts and self-talk soothe painful thought loops we find ourselves caught in, setting our minds free.

While practising kinder self-talk, like any art, takes patience and effort, the rewards are infinite. A kinder inner voice creates spaciousness in our hearts and minds. It allows us to look at ourselves lovingly, and give ourselves the tenderness and compassion we need to know and care for ourselves fully. Kinder thinking elevates and soothes us, allowing us to rest, relax and enjoy life.

Thinking kind thoughts is not complicated: it is a simple, natural choice available to each and every one of us, in every moment. When we begin with kindness towards ourselves, we actively choose love over fear. We cultivate mindfulness and positivity in daily life. We see that life becomes easier when we are kind to ourselves, and that the pieces of ourselves we thought were lost begin to return home to us at last.

Punishing and criticising ourselves never gets us where we want to be. On the contrary, we grow far stronger and wiser through our kindness. Kindness towards ourselves nurtures the confidence and peace of mind we seek to possess. With peace of mind and confidence we move more easily forward in our lives, thinking consistently kinder, healthier and more useful thoughts over time. All the joys this life has to offer open up to us with a kinder inner voice as our compass.

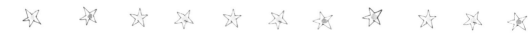

TRANSFORMING OURSELVES WITH KINDNESS

Transforming ourselves for the better need not be a painstaking or complicated process. Simple, fun practices inspired by kindness result in deep, lasting personal changes.

When we put ourselves down with our self-talk, we engage in a kind of internal warfare. This warfare is usually underpinned by illusions about our 'not-enoughness'. We may tell ourselves we are not good enough, deserving enough, smart enough, strong enough, pretty enough, accomplished enough, or that we have failed somehow ... the list goes on. Such unkind self-talk leads to unnecessary and unwanted feelings of anxiety, worthlessness, negativity and fatigue. The internal warfare we actively engage in with our unkind self-talk, be it wittingly or unwittingly, only serves to hurt and diminish us.

Regardless of what our inner voices may currently declare, the best news is that we are free to change and choose what we hear. We are free to put our weapons down and surrender to ourselves immediately, and at last. When we crowd our unkind thoughts out with kind ones, we begin. With our daily effort, we soon find that our pool of thoughts has completely changed to accommodate who we really are inside, and facilitate the lives we truly want to live.

When we are kind to ourselves, we stop struggling to be who we aren't or to 'fit in' at our own expense. Instead, we set ourselves free to be and enjoy who we are. As the poet and author Maya Angelou reminded us, the highest success we can achieve in this life is liking ourselves, liking what we do and liking how we do it. Kindness towards ourselves is a sure path to this wonderful state of being.

Crowding out unhelpful, unkind thoughts is a process that works over time rather than a snap-boom transformation. The art of crowding out unkind thoughts simply involves thinking more kind thoughts. It also involves intercepting unkind thoughts as they happen, even if this feels strange to begin with. For example, the thought 'I'm not successful enough' can be intercepted and replaced with 'I can see all that I've achieved'. The thought 'I'm not beautiful enough' can be replaced with 'I feel beautiful, whole and complete'. Crowding out and replacing unkind thoughts with kind ones is an enjoyable personal challenge that at the start may seem unnatural, but is simply a routine matter of reprogramming our software. We must persist with dedication! When we aim for progress, not perfection, we allow more room for kindness to change our lives.

Our brains are machines that take in, store and output information using neural pathways. When we crowd out unkind thinking with kind thinking, we simply stop using well-worn but useless neural pathways, pathways that no longer serve us, and we create new, healthy and supportive ones. With commitment and practice, our old, unwanted pathways will eventually dissolve and our new ones will effortlessly take precedence. Our minds organically favour these kind new pathways we have created because of our dedicated practice and repetition, but also because they make us feel exponentially better, mind, body and spirit.

Finding motivation to continue with and commit to our kindness practice will not be hard, as the side-effects of kindness are so tangible, rewarding and uplifting. For more inspiration and some refreshing examples of transformative thinking, turn to pages 66–67.

KINDNESS AND LITTLE THINGS

When it comes to real, joyous and lasting self-transformation, it is the small changes and cumulative kindnesses we do unto ourselves that seem to be most effective.

Big 'night and day' transformations are not always the ones that stick for good, as while something externally may seem changed in an obvious or dramatic way, we may remain unchanged deep within.

There is so much to be said for little, manageable kindnesses towards ourselves made regularly: positive little rituals or routines that we commit to in daily life. In the repetition of such uplifting and loving acts, our commitment to kindness is strengthened, and the life-changing shifts we wish to see slowly but very surely manifest. A kinder attitude towards ourselves gifts us patience as we grow and change, while a kinder inner voice offers us limitless support and positive reinforcement.

So where can we begin? We might commit to reciting one positive affirmation a day. Writing in our gratitude journals at night. Routinely unplugging from our devices. Dedicating a few minutes to our breath or meditation each morning. Smiling at ourselves when we look in a mirror. Scheduling time for regular exercise we actually enjoy. Choosing healthy, delicious foods to nurture us day to day. Noticing the stars at night, or the colours and moods of the sunrise or sunset. Timeless wisdom suggests that we are what we repeatedly do. Little things matter.

When it comes to our personal transformations, we need to think not only about who we will be and how we will feel tomorrow, but who we will be and how we will feel a year from now. Five or ten years from now. Let us allow ourselves such time and space to see just how profound small, habitual kindnesses towards ourselves can be, and savour the lifelong joy of our transformations.

No act of kindness,
no matter how small,
is ever wasted.

✫

Aesop

AVOIDING THE SNOWBALL

It is wise to pay attention to our thoughts and self-talk in the face of any so-called 'failure', or setback. Mostly unwittingly and at an alarmingly rapid rate, we can exacerbate personal challenges by adding a totally unhelpful array of other, unrelated stories to them. For example, we may fail at a single, particular test and suddenly we are hopeless, terrible and incapable people. We may unintentionally let somebody down and all at once we are unreliable, inconsiderate failures in all aspects of our lives. We may have one or two failed romances and declare ourselves utterly unlovable people, destined to live alone for the rest of our lives, communicating only with our pets!

When we create snowballs, we swiftly conjure up all sorts of evidence against ourselves as we wallow in our disappointment. We compound our suffering with our own stories and associations. Snowballing, particularly at times in our lives when the last thing we need is further discouragement, is truly unhelpful and unkind behaviour.

We have to contain ourselves. Rather than seeing our failures and enlarging them with our own unhelpful additives, we can choose not to make snowballs. Rather than drawing sweeping, unproductive and unkind conclusions about our whole selves based on individual experiences of 'failure'; and rather than questioning our entire worth, talent, potential and ability with every setback we experience, we can isolate the actual act, moment or circumstance at hand, and focus on it individually. Perhaps we made a mistake, or received negative feedback. Neither of these happenings determines our overall value or capability, but both invite us to do things differently next time. We're simply being offered a chance to improve ourselves for the future. Indeed, failures are inevitable when we step outside our comfort zones to learn new things and lead passionate, expansive and interesting lives. If we were never to make mistakes, we would never grow.

At age sixteen, Albert Einstein failed an exam to enter a Swiss school at which he endeavoured to study. He later struggled his way through university, becoming so demoralised that he almost dropped out. Heartbreaking for Albert, and unfathomable for us today, knowing that he went on to bring us the theory of relativity, among many other things. The idea of life is not to be perfect, or to master things immediately, but to try to do a little better tomorrow than we did today. We all try our best, learn and grow. Let's be kind to ourselves, each step of the way.

ACCEPTANCE
OF OURSELVES
SURRENDERS US TO
THE PEACE AND
RELAXATION WE
DESERVE TO KNOW.

m

KINDNESS AND OUR BODIES

Our bodies are our living, breathing homes: wise, miraculous ecosystems with thoughts, feelings and memories of their own. Our bodies love us, and want us to love them back.

Over time, a culture of perfectionism has flourished through visual media, the effects of which have been all-pervasive. People seem to be more anxious, pressured and self-conscious in their bodies than ever before. The joy of actually living in our bodies comes second to how our bodies look. We find ourselves striving in vain for a make-believe idea of 'perfection'. We cannot compare our real selves to digitally enhanced bodies, faces and lives and expect to feel content.

Perfectionism could be described as unkindness towards ourselves. It puts us under immense and unnecessary pressure, underestimates our intelligence, and undermines our true value as human beings. More than ever, we need to focus on being present, not perfect. We can be so caught up in appearances that we are miles away from ourselves, and from the pleasure of the moment.

If you find yourself berating or punishing your body for a 'picture perfect' result, stop and take a step back. Real wellness, peace and beauty are never found through punishment, suffering and deprivation. They are met only on paths inspired by love, peace and celebration.

If you are in a strained and difficult relationship with your precious body, where can you begin? Embrace your body and mind with simple practices of self-care in daily life. Shift your focus towards what your heart is trying to tell you. Listen gently and carefully to yourself. Take your time. Be compassionate. Pay attention to your thoughts and self-talk. Find sassy, fun ways to talk back to your inner critic, or alternatively crowd out your unkind, unhelpful thoughts with better quality ones. Most importantly and quite simply, ask to be shown the ways back to love and to kindness. No matter what hiccups or setbacks you may endure on your path of healing self-care, keep asking in faith. You will be heard, and you *will* be shown the way.

When we love our whole selves, mind, body and soul, with kindness, we come into balance. From this place we can intuitively make day-to-day decisions in support of our natural health and wellness, and find healthy moderation and pleasure in all areas of our lives. At the end of our days, we will no doubt feel more grateful to have loved, lived and celebrated ourselves and our bodies rather than having perpetually suffered our own unkindness and disapproval.

We need to be part of a positive revolution by being unconditionally kind towards our bodies. By loving our bodies with abundant healthy food, water, fresh air, sunshine, movement, compliments, rest and play. By luxuriating, enjoying and treating our bodies to pleasures of all kinds, we allow ourselves and others to feel we are enough. To feel happy, whole and beautiful, just as we are.

Kindness involves respecting the diversity of body shapes and sizes, yours and others. It is life-changing to realise that self-love, self-confidence, inner peace, and a smile that emanates from within will always be our most precious beauty accessories. When we cultivate kindness, our bodies will naturally look and feel more relaxed, nourished and at home; our faces will be softer, more welcoming and beautiful than ever before.

We cannot forget that at some point everything we love and have will disappear, including our physical bodies. This needn't make us sad; it should inspire us to fully appreciate the impermanence of all things, refresh our perspective about what really matters, and live fully in the moment. We cannot live in the past or the future and be happy. The only time we actually have to be happy is now. We can take up home in our bodies and truly live, not with obsession, negativity or shame, but with real love, joy and wonder.

MY BODY
LOVES ME.

m

PERSONALISED INNER WISDOM

We are each gifted a personalised, in-built self-care system.
We need only pay attention to and acknowledge it in order to
experience it working for us, body and spirit. When we are tired,
stressed, irritable or feeling overstretched, or when we notice that
we are thinking, speaking or acting unkindly, we need to take rest
and refresh our spirits. We need to stop and tend to ourselves
with loving kindness.

We needn't begrudge, mask over or ignore challenging thoughts or feelings when they arise. We mustn't feel ashamed or guilty, nor compound our suffering with our own judgement. Instead, we can choose to thank our minds and bodies for the wisdom they so directly provide us, encouraging us to embrace positive changes through self-kindness and self-awareness.

Unpleasant states or feelings we experience can be seen as markers that our cups need filling, first and foremost, by ourselves for ourselves. We are the ones responsible for replenishing ourselves by ritualising kind and considerate self-care practices in daily life. We are the only ones who can practise self-care. No one else can 'do' self-care for us. And that's just as well. Because as it happens, the care we give to ourselves is the best and most precious we can get! Our care for ourselves will always be the most healing and sustaining care available to us.

The more often we connect with our personalised inner wisdom each day, the clearer it becomes and the stronger we grow. Simply by tuning into ourselves gently and being ready to listen for guidance from within, we access our wondrously precious, ever-present and ever-giving gift.

KINDNESS AND OUR EVERYDAY ROUTINES

We can bring kindness to anything and everything we do. While every day is different, there are certain kindnesses that must be non-negotiable daily rituals. We are called to commit to these rituals in order to love and support ourselves through life. In my eyes these practices involve mindful eating, joyous movement, showing love to our minds and bodies, exploring our intuition and creativity, resting, relaxing and connecting with others.

When we eat mindfully we nourish ourselves with healing sustenance. We eat a rainbow of nutrient-rich whole foods from nature, and we drink ample water to hydrate our cells. We take a vested interest in understanding the source, treatment and health benefits of the foods available to us, and we thank our earth for providing us with such divine, edible riches. When we eat mindfully, we practise true kindness towards our bodies, our minds and our earth. The food we eat becomes our blood, bones and all the cells of our bodies. We literally are what we eat. Offering loving attention towards our food choices and our food itself is a form of self-care, and an essential daily kindness.

Moving our bodies is also a kindness towards ourselves, as our bodies need and love to move! As we exercise we not only stretch, strengthen and re-energise our bodies, we calm and clear our minds. Through movement we come to know and trust our bodies more each day, and by choosing movement we enjoy, we benefit all the more from our pleasure. Enjoy whatever it is that moves you – from tai chi to trampolining, yoga to snorkelling! Physical exercise dispatches endorphins around our bodies, happy chemicals that make us feel great and assist in reducing stress and anxiety. All the more reason to get moving in a spirit of joy and appreciation!

I consider using our creativity and connecting with our intuition essential daily rituals, too, as when we honour our imaginations, we are kind to our minds. Our creativity refreshes, grows, frees and fulfils us. Bringing creativity to the work we do and the activities we choose to enjoy guarantees us daily upliftment. Be creative with the thoughts you think, the words you choose, the clothes you wear, the home you live in and the relationships you nurture. Think fresh ideas, perform creative, random acts of kindness, potter, daydream, breathe, meditate, and let your mind wander. By using our creativity each day we enhance our relationship with ourselves, connect with our intuition, reinvigorate our bonds with others, feel happier and healthier, and receive endless inspiration for life.

Likewise, rest and relaxation must be treasured, prioritised aspects of our daily routines. We all do so much, yet without rest, peace and quiet we cannot go on. Our lives are shaped from the inside out. Resting well nourishes our inner worlds, growing greater peace, self-awareness and flow. We may understand rest more deeply by turning back to nature for comfort and inspiration. In nature there are seasons for blossoming, shedding, growing and resting, and each season has its perfect place in a dynamic bigger picture. As the poet Ovid so beautifully reminds us, we need to rest in order to flourish. Just as a field that has rested gives a bountiful crop, with rest, we too will blossom.

With kindness and patience towards ourselves, we learn to view rest and downtime with fresh eyes. We come to see that our productivity does not define us, nor does it equate to our success. We learn to rest without guilt or excuse, worry or judgement. We rest to connect with ourselves and our inner wisdom, to revitalise our minds and our bodies, and to fortify, heal and energise ourselves for daily life. For more words on kindness, rest and relaxation turn to page 56.

Last but not least, connection with others is a daily ritual that speaks to kindness in every way. When we really connect with each other through kind thoughts and kind actions, we honour, motivate and inspire each other for life. Active listening, tenderness, compassion, humour, understanding and empathy all activate and nurture meaningful connections: connections that make our lives rich and complete.

Be kind to yourself and others as a daily habit. You'll soon marvel at the richness of your life, and the joy you can bring to those with whom you share your world.

SUGAR, CAFFEINE AND KINDNESS

We might have become accustomed to propping ourselves up with sugar and caffeine to keep us upright and moving forward.

Good luck to anyone who'd dare try conversing with us before our morning coffee, and by 3 pm we would probably run naked down the street for a sweet biscuit! The trouble is, sugar and caffeine can have us running on adrenalin, masking the fact that we are running on empty inside.

The difficult thing about sugar and caffeine is that, while enticing, normalised and glamourised in the busy world in which we live today, they have roller-coaster-like trajectories, where the highs induced are equivalent to the slumps that follow. The only way to keep the high energy flowing when living this way is to reach for more coffee and more sugar, putting more stress on our nervous system, our cells, our moods, and, in truth, all parts of our lives. In a world fuelled on adrenalin, where erratic behaviour, aggression, tension, anxiety and burnout are very real, it is very logical to consider what we ingest on a daily basis as a kindness to ourselves – our minds and our bodies – and to others.

Refined sugar and caffeine affect our brain chemistry, and change our bodies at a cellular level. Blood sugar issues and reliance on sugar can lead to erratic moods, irritability, mental and hormonal disturbances, and even more serious illnesses such as diabetes. When living on an unending energy roller-coaster day to day, it becomes harder to relax, think clearly, and be kind to ourselves and others. In the throes of highs and lows, it is also harder to see and tend to our actual needs, for example the real, genuine tiredness we might be feeling inside.

We all need extra energy in our lives. Indeed, living in this world requires our attention, courage and vitality. There are so many ways to build real energy for ourselves in daily life, approaches and resources that are kind and sustainable for our minds and bodies.

A few simple ideas that I love? I always make sure I am drinking plenty of water, getting enough light and fresh air, and moving my body as regularly as possible throughout the day. Sometimes it is these rudimentary but critical things our bodies are calling out for, not stimulants. I swap refined sugar for fresh or dried fruit, and avoid soft drinks, commercial baked goods, confectionery and various packaged products that contain very large amounts of sugar. Energy drinks are serious cause for concern, with a potent mix of caffeine and sugar. Our wise, generous minds and bodies were not designed to be 'turbocharged' so intensely and artificially.

Matcha green tea is a great coffee alternative with less caffeine, and health benefits to bedazzle. I call on adaptogenic herbs that help support my body, especially my adrenal glands, gently but surely giving me all the energy I need. Examples include tulsi tea, maca powder, herbal tonics incorporating ashwagandha and rhodiola, and medicinal mushrooms such as reishi, chaga, lion's mane and cordyceps. And this is just to name a few. There is a world of exciting options, both energising and delicious, to explore. If these suggestions sound foreign please do not be discouraged. I had to learn about these alternatives too, and feel truly grateful every day that I took the time to do so.

Supporting our energy and our wellness in kind, sustainable ways is wonderful not only for us, but also for others we live with and love. Our bodies love us back when we take the time to learn more about them and care for them, and our loved ones will love us all the more too, as we quite simply become happier, calmer, more grounded people.

A LITTLE NOTE ON KINDNESS, REST AND RELAXATION

Each time we choose to be calm and quieten our minds and bodies,
we perform acts of kindness towards ourselves.

At the fast pace of our lives, and in a time in which we are so 'switched on', switching off and relaxing are not luxuries; they are necessities. Exhaustion, time poverty and sleep deprivation are almost worn as badges of honour nowadays, stressing our collective need to reframe rest. The experience of 'burnout' is an epidemic of our era, but it can be circumvented through the gentle practice of kindness towards ourselves in daily life.

In the fast-moving world we now live in, productivity and achievement are too often championed over quality rest and inner peace. At worst, rest is seen as optional or as weakness, relaxation as indulgence. Yet without rest and relaxation, we simply cannot be our best selves. We cannot think clearly, make good decisions, focus, feel vital, solve problems or garner healthy perspective moment to moment. By habitually ignoring our inner calls for rest we ensure that we will feel frazzled, compromised and overwhelmed. Such stressed and strained states are precursors to all sorts of undesirable and unkind thoughts, words and actions.

Rest and relaxation do not equate to idleness. Indeed, we should never feel guilty or apologetic about taking rest. When we slow down to acknowledge and care for ourselves, we take stock of our lives and rejuvenate our spirits. We need to switch off from all interruptions as often as we can to fully partake in our relationships, and to be mindfully present to ourselves and the world around us. As an act of kindness, towards ourselves first and foremost but also to others, we need to rest often, and rest well. We are called to support ourselves unconditionally with kindness, and enjoy the downtime we need and deserve in daily life.

We cannot find time to rest or relax in daily life; we must make the time. Sleeping, taking short naps, meditating, putting our feet up, reading for pleasure, writing in our journals, forgoing social activities to savour some peace and quiet time at home, listening to music, indulging in a candlelit bath, enjoying gentle movement and being in nature are just a few ways to recharge our batteries for life. The practice of kindness is itself deeply relaxing, as being kind to ourselves and others nourishes and calms us. Take time to settle down and ground yourself gently. Recalibrate, think kinder thoughts, be grateful, rest. Just *be*, just as you are.

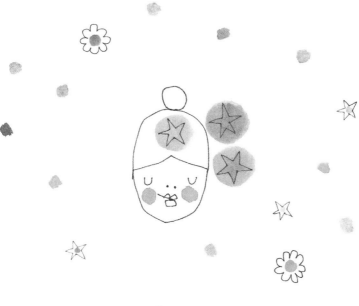

KINDNESS AND OUR ONLY CONSTANT: CHANGE

No flower is in bloom all year round. Nature takes rest. Leaves
fall from trees. Sunshine melts snow. Indeed, we are all part of
a bigger picture. Our shifting moods and states connect us to
the constant moods, weather, movement and renewal of nature.
We needn't judge the changing inner seasons we experience;
they constitute and enrich us.

It is nice to get curious about the ebb and flow of our feelings, and more fluid
with the endless changes we experience in and around us. Nothing stays the same,
and practising kindness towards ourselves helps us move with change.

When we practise self-acceptance through kindness, we integrate and welcome
home all parts of ourselves as dynamic, balanced and complete human beings.
When we model kindness towards ourselves in this way, we encourage those with
whom we share our world to do the same.

Some days we need patience; others, strength. Some days we need tenderness;
others, focus and determination. Relationships, experiences and circumstances in
our lives constantly shift and move us. Yet in the face of constant change, looking
upon ourselves with kindness is an anchoring practice that makes us feel more
at home within ourselves. Acceptance of ourselves in all our colours and seasons
surrenders us to the peace and relaxation we deserve to know.

We are never the same people going through the same experiences from one day to
the next. Life is ever-changing by nature, and we as human beings are on journeys
of constant personal growth. As the ancient Greek philosopher Heraclitus wisely
reminds us, we never step in the same river twice, because it is not the same river,
and we are not the same people.

BREATHE

REST

BE KIND

SAYING 'NO' WITH GRACE

We too often tend busily to the needs of others at the expense of our own. Yet it is only when we take care of ourselves fully that we are truly able to take care of others. There is nothing selfish about looking after ourselves as a matter of priority; it is an essential act of kindness. After all, we cannot pour from empty cups!

Through practising kindness towards ourselves we grow our ability to look after ourselves in any situation. We develop a baseline of reliable energy, and fortify a sense of self-confidence to strengthen and empower us for life. When we are kind to ourselves, we take the time to know ourselves and meet our needs in a deeper, more loving and encouraging way. We also become more attuned to our inner voice, our intuition. We begin to notice with greater clarity things to which we are naturally drawn, and others from which we turn away. We come to distinguish which ideas, activities and people align with our values and purpose, and which do not. Quite simply, in choosing kindness towards ourselves, we may determine what works and doesn't work for us, what feels good and what doesn't, and freely allow others to do the same.

We needn't deplete ourselves in the name of kindness towards others by overextending or overcommitting ourselves. We need not suffer in the name of kindness, nor allow our kindness to expose us to being overrun or mistreated. On the contrary, we are kindest to ourselves when we structure and respect boundaries that nurture and protect us, shaping our comfort, peace and safety in all situations and relationships.

It is important to see that we may be assertive while still being respectful and kind. We may say 'no' gracefully to things we do not wish to pursue while being kind. We may decline, refuse, offer constructive feedback or ask questions, all the while being thoughtful, loving and kind human beings. We can be generous while still protective of our personal time, space and energy.

While giving is one of life's most precious joys, it is not our job to complete anybody else, nor to heal them or make them happy. That is their own job. By practising and modelling self-care, we kindly encourage others to honour and support themselves first too.

Taking personal responsibility for our own health and happiness is an act of kindness not only towards ourselves, but towards all those with whom we share our lives. Kindness is by nature respectful. The tenderness and insight that kindness brings to ourselves, others, and all aspects of our lives is a welcome relief.

KINDNESS AS A SUPERPOWER — SOFTNESS AS STRENGTH

There is nothing so courageous, powerful or disarming as kindness, especially unexpected kindness in the face of injustice, meanness or judgement. When we practise the art of kindness, gentle yet effective approaches to get where we strive to be seem to appear, illuminated, before us. We realise quite clearly that kindness is not weak or passive — it is a form of superpower.

When we choose kindness we immediately do ourselves a great favour, and then allow the ripple effects of our positive choices to extend outwards. We can experience gentle, thoughtful and kind behaviour as strength in both our relationship with ourselves and in our bonds with others. Every time we choose compassion, peace, forgiveness, patience or inclusion, kindnesses readily available to us, we elevate ourselves and each other.

As the poet Kahlil Gibran wrote, tenderness and kindness are not signs of weakness and despair, but manifestations of strength and resolution. Indeed, cultivating a foundation of kindness allows us to be self-assured, ambitious and brave in daily life, and in such a way that powerfully honours ourselves and others.

There is no need for us to become aggressive, unkind or forceful to get our way. When we choose an aggressive approach in any exchange or situation, we inevitably do so at our own and others' expense. In contrast, when we have big dreams and perform great actions with kindness, we cannot help but respect and uplift ourselves and those around us.

Kindness is often associated with softness, a quality sometimes perceived as weakness. While kindness may be soft in some senses, especially considering that higher love is inherently gentle, softness has a triumphant, miraculous strength of its very own. Kindness can heal hurts, inspire forgiveness, grow self-esteem, bring balance and connect people of all kinds. Kindness can overcome fear, resolve disputes, re-establish harmony and change the world as we know it.

I hope the exercises and inspirations on the following pages will help you experience kindness as a joyous and uplifting form of self-care in your daily life.

I hold my heart out first,
like a lantern that lights my path.
I travel with my spirit for a compass,
my mind a budding flower.
I float through time
unencumbered by judgement
and open to love.

m

AFFIRMATIONS TO TRANSFORM OUTWORN THINKING

I'm not good enough.	I always do my best, and my best is good enough for me.
Other people are better than me.	My way of doing things is unique to me. I value myself and others.
I don't know what I want.	I'm finding my own way through life at my own pace. I'm being myself.
My body doesn't look how it should, or how I want it to.	My beautiful body is mine to nurture, enjoy and compliment. I take care of my body lovingly and as a matter of priority.

I've made so many mistakes. Why begin again now?	I love myself unconditionally and support myself to begin again, every time.
I shouldn't shine brightly.	I deserve to shine, and I allow others to do the same.
I shouldn't rest.	I rest and relax daily. When I'm rested I can take real joy in all that I am, and all that I do.
I'm not a good person.	I know myself. I have a good heart, and I want to use it to uplift myself and others.
I'm not doing life right.	I am courageous in living my life. I find peace and balance through constant kindness.
I don't deserve to feel proud of myself.	I see and celebrate all that I've achieved. I am free to approve of myself.

I RELEASE YOU.

I FORGIVE YOU.

I LOVE YOU.

m

MIRROR MIRROR!

Research has shown that twenty-one days (or three weeks) is an effective period of time in which to action a positive, new change. After that, it takes loving kindness towards ourselves to maintain it. This is a simple twenty-one-day exercise, helping you to grow in kindness towards yourself. I hope you will take it on, enjoy it, and let it change your life.

With each week, the normality of this exercise will increase, making it feel less strange. So please, persevere through the first couple of days in week one. I too felt uneasy looking in a mirror this way at first, but by week three, I was able to see myself for what felt like the first time in my life. I wish you joy and support in this exercise.

WEEK ONE. Each time you look in a mirror, before anything else, before any other words or thoughts, just say hello to yourself. You might find an awkward little pause after this hello. Take a nice breath with this pause and continue on with your day. Do this for seven days. Every time you see your reflection in a mirror or window, just say 'Hello', take a breath, and keep moving.

WEEK TWO. Each time you look in a mirror this week, before anything else, before any other words or thoughts, say 'Hello [your name]' and look yourself in the eyes. You might find a little pause after this greeting, or find your eyes hard to meet in the mirror. Breathe, smile gently, and continue on. Do this for seven days, every time you see your reflection in a mirror or window: say 'Hello [your name],' make eye contact with yourself, breathe, smile gently, and continue on with your day.

WEEK THREE. Each time you look in a mirror this week, before anything else, any other words or thoughts, just say 'Hello [your name], I love you.' You might find a profound pause after this statement. Take that moment to look yourself in the eyes, breathe and smile. Do this for seven days, every time you see your reflection in a mirror or window. Immediately say 'Hello [your name], I love you', look yourself in the eyes, breathe and smile gently. When you are ready, continue on with your day.

JOURNAL PROMPTS

To me, kindness means ...

Kindness makes me feel ...

I currently show myself kindness by ...

The things I enjoy about being me are ...

The achievements that I am proud of include ...

Aspects of my nature that I admire are ...

Parts of my body that I love are ...

Parts of my life that I love include ...

I can be kinder to myself by ...

I can be more patient with myself by ...

Thoughts and feelings I want to experience
more of in my daily life include ...

POSITIVE AFFIRMATIONS

Kindness makes me feel good.

Kindness expands my joy.

Kindness nourishes my mind.

Kindness grows good energy.

Self-care is self-love.

I HAVE A NURTURING,
NOURISHING RELATIONSHIP
WITH MY BEAUTIFUL BODY.

MY MIND AND BODY WORK
LOVINGLY TOGETHER IN
PERFECT HARMONY.

I LIBERATE MYSELF TO LIVE A
TRULY SATISFYING LIFE, RICH
IN PLEASURES OF ALL KINDS.

I MAKE TIME EACH DAY TO
MEET MY OWN NEEDS.

I DROP DOWN WITH EASE
FROM MY BUSY HEAD INTO
MY FEELING HEART.

MEDITATION

I close my eyes and take a quiet moment for myself now,
breathing deeply and slowly, in and out.
I watch my breath like waves, going out and coming back to shore.
As I slow and deepen my breathing, I calm and quieten my mind.

Breathing deeply in, I feel good when I am kind.
Breathing out, kindness brings me joy.

Breathing in deeply again, I relax when I am kind.
Breathing out slowly, I allow myself to blossom.

Breathing in, I honour myself with tenderness.
Breathing out, I know my body loves me.

Breathing in, I bathe in kindness.
Breathing out, I feel peace at last.

CONNECTIVE KINDNESS

LIFE-CHANGING KINDNESS IN ACTION

A little kindness can change a life in an instant. We underestimate our ability to transform somebody else's day with a word of encouragement, a wink or a smile, a good cup of tea delivered with love, a thoughtful acknowledgement, compassionate listening, a well-placed compliment, a helping hand, a hug, a thoughtful surprise or a random act of kindness.

In the words of Mother Teresa, 'Spread kindness wherever you go. Let nobody come to you without leaving happier.' Each and every little kindness counts; no gesture of acknowledgement or care for another person is too small. We must never miss our chance to say a nice word or take a kind action.

For example, we might look at a perfect stranger, a friend or a loved one in any given moment and think about how well they are doing; how generous or kind they are, or how beautiful they look. While we think these lovely things in our minds, we might not speak them in words. Yet kindness calls us to say good things out loud, spreading more joy, confidence and peace around us. When we acknowledge the efforts, beauty, achievements and talents of others, we honour and motivate them. We also feel a gorgeous, healing lightness within ourselves when we are kind towards others, as we sense our love coming full circle. If we were all to celebrate one another lovingly and build each other up with our kindness, we could together put an end to the joyless, competitive comparison in daily life.

Plato wrote of being kind in all exchanges. He suggested that others are usually suffering more than we are, and are always deserving of our care and respect. Be willing to help others through kindness, from loved ones to colleagues to perfect strangers. You never know – you might be the only one who makes that person feel good that day! It could also be that your kindness is more unforgettable and influential for them than you could ever know.

A friend of mine is a gardener. Her nails are often dark with soil, the palms of her hands well worn with work. She told me how she would often look at her hands, lamenting how weathered they looked. While out shopping one day, a lady noticed her hands and told her how beautiful they were. How they seemed to tell stories. It was only in that moment, in the experience of that kindness, that my friend was able to see her hands as beautiful. Somebody had taken the time to show her their appreciation and, in turn, inspired her to appreciate herself. Even the parts of ourselves that we worry about, negate, ignore or dislike – we can love these parts of us with kindness and bring them home.

Kindness in daily life involves the support and celebration of others: their stories, achievements and dreams. There is a reason for our being here, and there is enough space for all of us. Others' flourishing does not diminish our own. Be kind to others, and celebrate them as you yourself wish to be acknowledged. Celebrate others' gains as well as your own, boost them, elevate them, and let their successes inspire you. As the saying goes, 'Comparison is the thief of joy.' Let you be you. Love and nurture yourself, and encourage those with whom you share your world to do the same.

ONE MOMENT
CAN CHANGE A
DAY, ONE DAY CAN
CHANGE A LIFE,
AND ONE LIFE
CAN CHANGE
THE WORLD.

Buddha

KINDNESS, TIME AND CARE IN RELATIONSHIPS

Human relationships are living, breathing things. Like all works in progress, they require our loving effort. With our attention, time and care, we give our relationships the very best chance to flourish. We face so many distractions in this busy, switched-on world. We are constantly drawn away from our present moment, ourselves and our loved ones. Kindness in relationships involves making quality time for meaningful connection, conversation and shared experiences. If we are not present in our lives for the people with whom we share them, we miss everything.

Practising kindness is essential when it comes to nurturing and enjoying healthy relationships. Little kindnesses in romantic relationships grow intimacy and keep the fire of love alive. Little kindnesses in friendships and family circles keep us feeling connected and appreciated. Kindness in business relationships is powerful too, as kindness enables better collaboration and allows people to feel more at ease with one another.

When it comes to cultivating kind and joyous interpersonal relationships, mutual effort is essential. Any relationship in which one party is doing all the giving is unsustainable. On the other hand, in relationships based on shared effort, each party delights in supporting and enriching the other. Real love, comfort and joy grow out of mutual respect, tenderness and care.

Close attention to our own behaviour and attitudes is a key ingredient to creating happy and healthy relationships with others. We cannot be unkind or ungenerous and expect another sort of treatment in return. To find peace and happiness in any relationship, first we must ourselves be what we are looking for in others. If we are looking for love, attention, respect, peace and kindness, we must begin by being actively loving, attentive, respectful, peaceful and kind.

When we sprinkle kindness liberally around us, we create the magical feelings of love and connection we seek in our relationships. These delicious feelings are at the very heart of meaningful living, and they make our lives rich, fulfilling and exciting. Indeed, kindness expands love in relationships, supporting bonds that enrich and inspire us throughout our whole lives.

We can commit to kindness in relationships through thoughtful, generous words and acts, through expressing our joy and gratitude, and by offering our most precious gifts to one another: our time and care. There are infinite, creative ways to enjoy little kindnesses in our daily connections with others. See pages 112–129 for inspiration.

NEVER LOSE A CHANCE

OF SAYING A KIND WORD.

William Makepeace Thackeray

KINDNESS AND LISTENING IN RELATIONSHIPS

Kind communication grows respect, peace and joy: essential ingredients in happy, healthy relationships. We are called to be kind in the choice, tone and delivery of the words we speak, realising that the way we say things is just as important as what we say. We never know how long words that we say might stay in somebody else's memory, be they encouraging or disparaging. While unkind words and actions create unrest and disharmony in our relationships, kind words and actions grow trust, self-esteem and connection. There is a special piece in relationships that is more important than speaking, however — and that is listening.

It has been noted that we human beings are granted two ears and one mouth, and they should be used in that ratio. That is, we must endeavour to listen twice as much as we speak. When we practise kindness we learn to genuinely care more about others, and we naturally become better, more engaged listeners. We take the time to really hear others as they express themselves. We don't always need to have a response or a solution to offer when we actively listen; in fact, most of the time we will find that the person talking is best equipped to answer their own questions as they speak. Rather, we listen just to listen, with open hearts and minds, and if we happen to feel we can offer support in a meaningful way afterwards, we may respectfully do so.

To listen with compassion and tenderness is higher love in action. We cannot underestimate our capacity to change somebody's life in an instant when we are truly present with them in kindness. This applies to people who we know very well (the ones we too easily neglect to really hear) or to perfect strangers we may meet on our paths. When we warmly and lovingly listen to others' concerns, we help them to make valuable observations and connections of their own. Kindness in listening empowers others to better understand and care for themselves.

We learn and grow so much through mindful listening in all our various relationships, from intimate and romantic connections to bonds with friends, family, colleagues and fellow travellers. In return, and when we are listened to so completely by another, we too may know how profound it feels to be acknowledged, seen and understood in this life.

KINDNESS IN WORDS
CREATES CONFIDENCE.
KINDNESS IN
THINKING CREATES
PROFOUNDNESS.
KINDNESS IN GIVING
CREATES LOVE.

Lao-Tzu

CONNECTION AND WELLBEING

Kindness connects us. Through kindness, we recognise our shared experiences and common humanity rather than our disconnection and differences. Kindness creates bonds that link us to others, allowing us to feel part of something greater and offering us a sense of belonging. Through practising kindness we focus on what we can give and share with each other, and see our ability to uplift our own lives and the lives of others. In this way, kindness is a viable answer to loneliness, especially nowadays when we find ourselves more 'connected' yet 'disconnected' than ever before.

While we are ever-available via our various devices and may link up with others instantaneously, meaningful connection in real time has greatly diminished. It seems that people have been feeling sadder and more alone than ever before. In the face of such disconnection, it is heartening to acknowledge that simple words or acts of kindness possess the power to heal and unite us.

Our sense of connection with others affects our health and longevity. Like food, water and shelter, feelings of belonging in loving relationships, family circles, friendships and communities, are critical to our wellness. Loneliness and isolation

pose real health concerns, depressing our hearts, diminishing our vitality and weakening our immune systems. In some of the 'blue zones' on our earth (places in which significant numbers of inhabitants live above one hundred years of age), connection is acknowledged as key. Singing, dancing, gardening, cooking, and pooling funds and resources together are daily practices. People are imbued with a sense of purpose and meaning within such community. Young and old people alike are needed, valued and appreciated.

The art of kindness is not only a virtuous lifestyle, it is a healthy, generous, community- and life-affirming one too. When others care for us, think of us, include us, want to bring out the best in us and we in them, we decrease our individual and collective stress, pain and loneliness. We feel happier, more harmonious and motivated as we share the many pleasures life has to offer together. Joyous connections keep us feeling youthful, purposeful and alive. It is no wonder that connective kindness increases our vitality, immunity, and mental and physical health. It is indeed so healing and profound to give and receive kindness that it's an art deserving of our utmost care.

KINDNESS AND RECONNECTION

Each time we are kind, we contribute to a collective experience
of wellbeing and harmony on earth. If each one of us were to live
more kindly in love and respect for others, the world would be
a very different place. Simple acts of kindness – such as smiling,
offering someone a seat, asking if someone is okay, lending
a helping hand, initiating a conversation with someone,
or including someone on the outer – are powerful acts
that restore our faith in life and each other.

How can we begin reconnecting with each other in kindness? We can grow kindness by choosing to prioritise peace and harmony in all our relationships and, with mindful attention to others, be truly present in the precious time we get to spend with them. We can focus on tenderness and togetherness rather than competition, judgement or difference. We can highlight our shared need for downtime, rest and relaxation over incessant busy-ness, and support each other as we simplify and ease our paths. We can grow through kindness by making meaningful, close connections in the present moment, not only mediated connections across space and time. We can call rather than text, write occasional handwritten letters rather than rely solely on email, or make time to visit someone in person and experience real 'face time' together with them.

Looking into each other's eyes is a profound way we can connect with one another. We have become almost afraid of direct eye contact. It makes us feel vulnerable. Our eyes are the windows to our souls and they say so much. The immensity of really seeing another person in their fullness, and seeing ourselves reflected in their eyes, can be an overwhelming and emotional experience for us. Yet we must be brave and choose to see. Looking into one another's eyes with loving kindness is courageous, generous and transformative.

Paths back to one another are simple. They are not hard to find. We all need kindness, no matter who or where we are, how young or old, how independent or vulnerable, how up or down we may be. Acknowledgement and connection are essential to our health and happiness. We cannot think that, one day, when we have more time, more energy, more money, or more inspiration, that we will then make time to connect or reconnect with others. That only then will we be able to give to others. The only time we truly have to act is now, right here, in the present moment. The past has gone and the future is never guaranteed. Do not pass life or people by because you are too busy, or because you have lost sight of what matters. Be present in this life with kindness as your inspiration, and notice how much more alive you can feel.

TO BE KIND IS
MORE IMPORTANT
THAN TO BE RIGHT.
MANY TIMES WHAT
PEOPLE NEED IS NOT
A BRILLIANT MIND
THAT SPEAKS BUT
A SPECIAL HEART
THAT LISTENS.

Buddha

KINDNESS IN THE FACE OF CHALLENGE

Even, or especially, in the face of unkindness or disappointment, we are called to choose kindness. This is first and foremost for our own peace of mind and healing – an act of easing our own way – but it also releases others and prevents more suffering.

Indeed, there is nothing like unanticipated kindness to put a full stop on a lingering dispute, and at best it may forge a much-needed reconnection. There is no defence against kindness. It is irrefutable! Kindness does not weaken us; quite the contrary, it allows us to be stronger, calmer and more peaceful human beings.

When we are unkind, or when we ourselves are the recipients of unkindness from another, we are called to see what lies beneath the unkindness. Unkindness is like the tip of an iceberg. What lies beneath is the cold hardness of great pain and suffering. With this awareness, it suddenly seems much more possible for us to feel tenderness and compassion towards others acting unkindly. This insight can immediately shift our perspective, and change our course. When it comes to interpersonal rifts, the misguided ideas that retribution equates to closure, or that we have to 'be cruel to be kind', are hopeless. The simple truth is, we have to be kind to be kind.

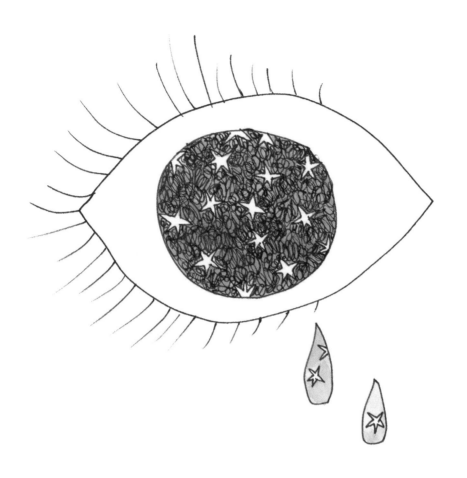

AN EYE FOR AN EYE
AND THE WHOLE
WORLD IS BLIND.

Mahatma Gandhi

It goes without saying that there are times in which it takes enormous inner strength to be kind. When we are hurt or wronged, we might feel tempted to be unkind in return. Yet putting one wrong atop another only compounds our problems. As Mahatma Gandhi reminds us, an eye for an eye and the whole world is blind. We move through life more easily and joyously by choosing kindness, grace and integrity every time. Forgiveness or compassion might seem like prickly or impossible options in the face of certain challenges, but when we choose to be unkind or unforgiving, we only hurt and exhaust ourselves more. On the contrary, we do ourselves and others a kindness in releasing our tensions and grudges, and transcending any fussy, worldly trappings that hold us back from love.

In moments when being kind may not seem immediately possible, we can simply choose not to be unkind. We can take a breather, reflect and decompress. In this space we create for ourselves in the 'heat of the moment', we allow ourselves to feel our emotions on our own terms, to settle and gain perspective. The same gentle approach is extremely useful for accessing kindness in the face of exhaustion or disillusionment. In difficult times, choosing kindness is a simple, tremendously powerful and transformative act of courage; one that cannot help but lighten and ease our way forward. Words, thoughts or actions born from fear and anger are almost always regrettable. But when all is said and done, we will never regret words, thoughts or actions born out of love and kindness.

KINDNESS AND OPEN-HEARTEDNESS

Kindness calls for an open heart. It involves not just tolerating but accepting and respecting others. It means seeing richness in our inevitably different beliefs, feelings, thoughts, idiosyncrasies and ideas.

Unkindness or judgement towards others because they disagree with us, do not share our attitudes or beliefs or are different from us exposes true small-heartedness within us. This small-heartedness will have a story of its own, and will ask for our own understanding, self-compassion and transformation.

Just as we can learn to intercept and change unkind thoughts that we think about ourselves, as if weeding the gardens of our minds, we can learn to do the same in our relationships with others. When we find ourselves thinking, speaking or acting unkindly towards others, we are called to apologise immediately and ask for forgiveness. We can pause, breathe, and simply say, 'I'm sorry. Please forgive me.' This humbling and life-changing practice grows stronger, more fulfilling relationships, makes us courageously vulnerable, and exemplifies the art of kindness as healing, higher love.

I'm sorry.
I crave peace too.
I want to better
understand
and love you.

Thank you,
but I am looking after myself.
I cannot say yes,
but I wish you well.

I can see you are hurting.
How can I comfort you?
Please let me show you
how much I care.

PATIENT KINDNESS

Living kindly grows our patience, and greater patience means
happier living. We have so many moments in life that require
our patience. When we are unwell and recuperating, when we
are waiting in a line, when we are waiting on a decision,
on a person, an event or a service, when we are disappointed,
held up or inconvenienced. To any such situation, kindness
brings much-needed ease, flow and peace.

While waiting on hold or in a queue, rather than becoming increasingly inflamed by
our impatience, we can think about all the other people in that queue. All the things
they need to do in their day. All the things that they have ever done in their lives.
All the feelings they must feel, commitments they must have, dreams they must hold
inside. Everyone has their place here, and one person's time is just as important as
another's. Exercising patience is a kindness to ourselves and to those with whom we
share our world.

We can reframe disappointments, delays or challenges in our days as opportunities
to practise patience. Next time you are held up, take a moment to breathe in and out
mindfully rather than looking for a quick-fix distraction, filling every waiting moment
with new input. We are so accustomed to scrolling, checking our correspondence and
turning away from ourselves for entertainment that we lose sacred opportunities to
just be with ourselves, in our bodies, where we are. Practising kindness in this way,
we soon find that the 'in-between' moments in our days, ones that require a little of
our time or patience, are great opportunities to reflect, slow down, daydream and,
most importantly, reconnect lovingly with ourselves.

COMPASSIONATE KINDNESS

Through kindness we grow our compassion: our ability to feel with and for others. Interestingly, the word 'compassion' literally means 'to suffer with' others, to sense what others are going through, and to be lovingly present with them. True compassion connects us with others in empathetic, non-judgemental and loving ways, no matter who or where we are. Rather than contributing to more fear, pain, disconnection and struggle through ignorance or unkindness, we can choose to be compassionate, tender, peaceful and respectful instead.

In the words of American civil rights activist Jesse Jackson, 'Never look down on anybody unless you're helping them up.' Each time we think, speak or act in unkindness, we weaken ourselves and each other. Each time we practise the art of kindness instead, we really see, fortify and support one another. We have a choice, and change begins with us.

There are some people in this world whose joys and freedoms are restricted by circumstances beyond our comprehension. It is our duty to send loving thoughts of kindness to all people each day, and to offer healing prayers of tenderness and

support for others. While loving thoughts and prayers may not seem like enough to turn the tide, they are in fact profound energetic actions that inspire change, and they are available to each one of us in every moment.

While it is natural to feel undeserving or challenged in the face of our privilege and others' pain, diminishing our joy serves nobody. Being sad because others are sad compounds our collective pain. Our compassion allows us to feel as human beings, empathising deeply with one another. Yet when we are kind to ourselves, we see that we needn't suffer in order to acknowledge and be actively compassionate towards others who are suffering. On the contrary, we are called to live full, rich lives in loving service of ourselves, others and our earth.

We are all connected, all people in all places. We are each made of the same cosmic matter. As poet and scholar Rumi reminds us, the entire universe is inside us all. We are made up of the past, present and future, and of all the secrets and mysteries of the universe. We lead different lives in vastly different worlds, and we make different choices for different reasons. Yet we all share the same innate humanness, our need to be loved.

When we actively commit to kindness in our immediate circles, we become part of a peaceful and loving solution on a larger scale. We choose empowerment in the face of suffering. By being kind in daily life, we grow compassion within and around us. We take personal responsibility for our energetic imprint in this world. If each one of us were to be compassionate for our own and each other's circumstances, the world as we know it would radically transform.

We need to see our value as individuals making positive change. We must hold tight, living and projecting kindness each day, and knowing that each and every one of us matters. We must never forget our call to love, nor underestimate how profoundly we can change the world.

This is my simple religion.
No need for temples.
No need for complicated
philosophy. Your own mind,
your own heart is the
temple. Your philosophy
is simple kindness.

Dalai Lama XIV

ACTS OF KINDNESS

Put kindness into action, and watch all parts of your life blossom.

KINDNESS IN OUR HOMES

INITIATIVE. Grow the connection, love and laughter in your home with all sorts of little kindnesses. A kind home is a happy home.

Take the initiative to do little jobs around the house without prompting, such as washing the dishes, sweeping the floor, making a cup of tea for a loved one, or making the bed with care.

MAKE YOUR HOME BEAUTIFUL. If you share your space, enlist the help of all people in the residence to keep it clean, tidy and uplifting. Arrange beautiful flowers to be enjoyed. Cook special meals to be savoured together. These needn't be fussy or complicated meals; simple is best. Set the table thoughtfully, and make any occasion a special one.

You might like to find out what your family members' favourite meals, activities, music, books or movies are. Enjoy these together with them if you can. Make an effort to bring them joy.

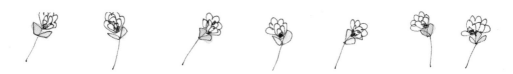

COMMUNICATION.

Make time each day to listen to your loved ones with your undivided attention. Set aside all distractions and listen actively without judgement or interruption. This practice allows your home to become a safe haven for openness and communication.

Write thoughtful love notes to your partner, children or housemates for no particular occasion, and dispatch them liberally. Never be backwards in coming forwards when it comes to showing your loving kindness.

Let your loved ones know if you'll be late or if you change your plans. They might be counting on you, and clear communication will show your respect for their time.

The language and tone we use to communicate our messages to loved ones is just as, if not more, important than the messages themselves! Being aware of our delivery makes a world of difference, and can circumvent unwanted tension, negativity and distress at home.

THOUGHTFULNESS.

Give genuine, creative compliments to your loved ones at home, especially ones you know will make them feel really good. We should never become so familiar with those closest to us that we forget to notice and admire them as they deserve. This sort of kindness matters so much.

Little things like laying out your loved one's pyjamas, putting a glass of water at their bedside or waking them up to a cup of tea are simple and free kindnesses that create a culture of generosity and care at home.

CARE. Greet each other upon rising and tucking into bed at night. Make yourself and your loved ones on-the-go lunch boxes to stay nourished throughout the day. Make happy rituals to mark your days. Organise themed nights or special celebrations, even if there's no particular occasion to mark. Choose to celebrate life just because.

MODELLING KINDNESS. Our home environments are schools of love, and our children learn kindness by osmosis. The best thing we can do at home is create a kind and loving space for ourselves and each other. Rather than focusing on our children's achievements and progress reports, we can divert our attention to the kindnesses in their days, the creative ideas they are growing, or the reasons they have for which to feel grateful. There is enough pressure in the world at large. We need our homes to be peaceful sanctuaries for our children where they are able to potter, play, and feel relaxed and free. After all, by raising kinder children, we pave the way for a kinder world.

A KIND
HOME IS
A HAPPY
HOME.

m

KINDNESS AT SCHOOL

INCLUSIVENESS. Schools can be grounds for unkindness and exclusion, but they are equally places where unforgettable, life-changing kindnesses can triumph. Make special effort to notice people who need to be included and welcome them in. Nobody should feel lonely. Just imagine how you would feel if you were the one on the outer. Choose kindness every time.

PRAISE. Notice the good in your friends and go to the extra effort of complimenting and praising them. Celebrate others' gifts and abilities. Take joy in the happiness of others as you would wish them to take joy in your own.

RESPECT. Be kind to fellow students and teachers. Everyone matters. Everyone's time and feelings matter.

INTEGRITY. Dismiss gossip and small talk. See yourself above such unkindness, and step aside to pursue higher conversation, thoughts and ideas.

KINDNESS AT WORK

INITIATIVE. Take initiative by offering your help and support to others without being asked. Everyone benefits from receiving support, yet few of us feel comfortable asking for it. Be attentive, and you will spot many valuable opportunities to offer your kindness and bring joy to others. You will soon find that others are more readily available to support you too.

CONNECTION. Colleagues, co-workers and support staff can pass one another in the corridor or lift daily, not knowing one another by name. We enrich our own and each other's lives when we care enough to greet one another and wish each other well. Looking up from our devices, making eye contact and saying hello are simple acts that make a world of difference.

Acknowledging the efforts of others in the workplace, offering genuine compliments or providing positive feedback are other ways to bring about more connection through kindness. A more connected workplace is always a happier, more successful one.

COMMITMENT. When we bring our passion and dedication to our work, we do kindness unto ourselves and others. Half-hearted work or begrudging effort will never change the world, or our lives, for the better. When you use your creativity and focus to make positive change you spread joy, no matter what you do. You will soon find more fulfilment, excitement and potential in your work and life.

KINDNESS IN OUR COMMUNITIES

GENEROSITY. Be generous with your time and energy wherever possible. Volunteer, be involved, share your resources and talents, and connect with younger and older community members alike in ways that uplift and inspire. There are always ways we can lend a hand. Check local papers, community boards and websites to find ways you can bring more kindness to your local community.

CREATIVITY. Be creative and come together in your community. Plan street parties, fundraising events, information or film screening nights. Find ways of swapping and sharing resources, pooling together so that less 'things' are required to meet your community's needs. You may have a lawnmower your neighbour doesn't have, but they may have a canoe you could borrow for an afternoon adventure! By being creative and kind, giving and receiving, we will inevitably discover all kinds of joys and conveniences. We will also have more reason to communicate and connect with our neighbours, share our lives together, and reap the feel-good benefits of community spirit.

KINDNESS IN OUR FRIENDSHIPS

ATTENTION. Friendships require time, energy and effort to flourish. Calling our friends and keeping in touch with them, letting them know they are being thought of, is very important. We need the same grace and support in our own lives too. Be aware of friends' circumstances and offer your encouragement as they pursue their goals and dreams. Call simply to say hello, or just to check if they're doing okay. Simple kindnesses such as these demonstrate care, and strengthen us all.

TOGETHERNESS. Wherever possible, have face time with people in real space and time. It is important that we balance friendships into our working weeks and family lives, as they are so very important to our health and happiness. Be kind and uplifting, and choose kind and uplifting people as friends. This way, getting together will always be a relaxing and joyous treat.

TENDERNESS. When we are available and open-minded as friends, we are great listeners and supporters for the people we care about. By showing our tenderness and care, our encouragement, empathy and understanding, or just by giving a good cuddle, we can soothe and comfort each other. As poet Ralph Waldo Emerson reminds us, we can never do a kindness too soon.

We cannot tell the precise moment when friendship is formed. As in filling a vessel drop by drop, there is at last a drop which makes it run over. So in a series of acts of kindness there is, at last, one which makes the heart run over.

James Boswell

KINDNESS ON THE GO

PATIENCE. Living in a busy, bustling world with others who have their own needs, hurries and worries requires our patience.

Be kind on the road. Leave a little earlier so you don't need to race or stress. Refrain from expressing your unresolved rage on the road and find ways to breathe through inconveniences. Let life go on.

When queuing, waiting for a person, service or event, practise kindness. Pushing, complaining and stress-making are exhausting unkindnesses to ourselves and others.

Let's treat others with the same tolerance we seek to know.

RESPECT. There are so many opportunities to be kind on the go. Show less-mobile passengers respect on public transport by offering them your seat before they can ask. Help someone up if they fall. Open a door, pull up a chair, greet others with a smile. If you're in a position to help, assist a person struggling to carry something heavy. If the person behind you has a few items at the market and you have a whole trolley, let them go before you.

OBSERVE. Being observant is part of being respectful. When we are observant, we notice all the more chances in daily life to ease the paths of others with whom we share our world. When such kindnesses are done unto us, we feel the joy of living. Let us be part of spreading this joy by actively showing our care and respect for one another.

TO HAVE A FRIEND
IS TO BE ONE.

Anon

JOURNAL PROMPTS

Some memorable moments of kindness in my life include ...

Some special compliments that I have received are ...

People who support my hopes and dreams include ...

These are some acts of kindness I have witnessed in life ...

Ways in which I have been kind to others include ...

Some random acts of kindness I would like to try are ...

These are some of my happiest moments to date ...

This is what compassion means to me ...

POSITIVE AFFIRMATIONS

Choosing kindness means growing happiness.

Kindness nourishes my spirit.

Kindness strengthens my relationships.

Kindness shapes my daily actions and words.

Love and friendship bless and fortify me.

My connections with others enrich my life.

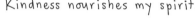
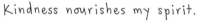
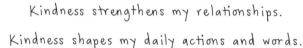
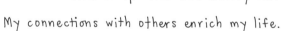

CHOOSING KINDNESS
TOWARDS OTHERS MAKES
ME HAPPY.

LIVING WITH GRATITUDE
PAVES MY WAY TO
ABUNDANCE AND JOY.

WHEN I LET GO,
I FEEL FREE.

I FIND PEACE IN
FORGIVENESS.

I FILL MY CUP FREELY
WITH ALL THE RICHES MY
LIFE HAS TO OFFER.

MEDITATION

Taking a moment for myself now, I close my eyes.
I slowly calm and quieten my breathing.
For a moment there is nothing for me to do,
nothing for me to think about.
I am just here,
breathing in,
and breathing out.
One breath after the other, I feel my body rise and fall.
Breathing in I notice new air fill my chest.
Breathing out I exhale old hurries and worries.
When I feel ready,
I take a moment to think about the people in my life,
people who make me feel good.
I see their faces and hear their voices.
They are showing me how much they love me.
I can see and hear them now.
Inhaling, I breathe in gratitude for friendship.
Breathing out, I feel the joy of laughter and togetherness.
Breathing in again now I inhale the feeling of love.
Exhaling I feel the warmth and light of love fill my body.

All the cells of my body, from the crown of my head
to the soles of my feet, are vibrating with lightness.

I breathe in and out from my heart now,
and I thank it for its kindness.
Slowly breathing into my heart,
and out from my heart.
One breath after the other.
I breathe more room in my heart for kindness
with each breath now.
I make space for more love.
In this quiet space I know that I am loved and lovable.
I am whole and complete.
As I gently open my eyes,
I feel my aliveness.
I sense all the love within and around me.

I know my heart is open.
I see my world as kind.

THOUGH THERE
MAY BE TIMES WHEN
YOUR HANDS ARE
EMPTY, YOUR HEART
IS ALWAYS FULL, AND
YOU CAN GIVE THINGS
OUT OF THAT — WARM
THINGS, KIND THINGS,
SWEET THINGS.

Frances Hodgson Burnett

KINDNESS TOWARDS OUR EARTH

BORROWING OUR EARTH

There is a Native American proverb, 'We don't inherit the earth from our ancestors, we borrow it from our children.' Being alive, really living, means offering tenderness and respect towards our earth and all her creatures. It means treading lightly and caring about not only the present but also the future of our planet. It means planting trees under whose shade we may never sit.

When we borrow something, the typical expectation is that we will return it in the same condition in which it was received. When we consider this notion and look at ourselves as present caretakers of this earth, we cannot say that we are honouring our collective responsibility. We take relentlessly from our earth, overdraw from her, and assume that her abundance will remain at our disposal. We assume by some miracle that she will remain happy and healthy for our sake, and for the sake of our children. Our user culture cannot sustain life on earth, yet we are blinded by our disconnection from nature, and our desire for more. We cannot forget that we are borrowing this earth from our children, and we need to learn how to be kind towards her.

Practising kindness is sometimes about taking initiative: going above and beyond with love when we identify the possibility to do so. In the words of Italian poet Dante Alighieri, 'He who sees a need and waits to be asked for help is as unkind as if he had refused it.' Indeed, we mustn't choose to ignore people, creatures or our beautiful earth by passing by or turning the other way. This itself constitutes unkindness, and in no way contributes to the wholeness and healing of life on earth. When it comes to our disturbing environmental and health concerns, we cannot refuse to worry because 'it won't happen in our time'. Kindness is proactive, wise, courageous and always possible. Kindness sees openings for greater love, and actively fills those spaces with hope.

WE DON'T
INHERIT
THE EARTH
FROM OUR
ANCESTORS,
WE BORROW
IT FROM OUR
CHILDREN.

Native American proverb

WONDER AND GRATITUDE

Our earth is spectacular and dynamic, vast and beautiful, living and breathing. Honouring our earth with our wonder is essential human kindness. How many starry nights or full moons have we missed, sunsets bypassed? How often do we take a moment to observe and admire our fellow living things such as plants and animals? How often do we miss the richness of the changing colours, shapes, sounds and sights of our environments because we are too busy, looking down, or mentally miles away from our present moment?

Noticing our earth is a kindness towards her, not to mention a gift to ourselves. Such kindness involves taking time to notice the little and big things about being alive; immersing ourselves in the elements, and appreciating the seasons, textures, sounds and sights surrounding us.

We can acknowledge the trees that oxygenate the air we breathe, or the water that satiates, purifies and energises us. We can see the force of the wind that clears our skies, or carries little seedlings upon itself to disperse and grow. We can be warmed by the side of a bonfire under the stars, or watch the way wildfire can ravage verdant land, only to see it regenerate triumphantly. We can notice the perfumes

of springtime, the bracing air on a winter's morning, the changing colours of autumn leaves, or the delicious warmth of summer sun.

When we stop to notice how miraculous and splendid our earth is, we are humbled. We realise that we simply cannot consciously continue to 'use' our earth, or take her for granted. We have nothing without the wellness of our planet, and we are called to love her. It is when we touch such love and gratitude for our earth that we are encouraged to make the changes we wish to see in this world.

It is important to see that we human beings are part of Mother Nature, not separate from or superior to her. Taking time to appreciate our natural environments with loving attention is itself a therapeutic, refreshing and restorative practice. In coming back to nature with kindness, we come lovingly back home to ourselves at last too. It is in nature that real healing begins, for us and for our earth.

WHEN WE BUY
WHAT WE DO NOT
NEED, WE STEAL
FROM OURSELVES.

Swedish proverb

KINDNESS AND CONSUMPTION

Our consumption has grown to epidemic proportions. We are consumers of media that encourage us to upgrade, upsize, buy and spend more. We buy more fast fashion, homewares and electronic gadgets, beauty products, flashy cars and extra unneeded things, becoming victims of advertising that appeals to our 'lack'. Our consumption is meant to make us happy, yet somehow we aren't.

Social media feeds our culture of comparison, fuelling our unending desire for more. We consume products with built-in obsolescence, items designed with short life spans that implore us to buy again. Enough never seems to be enough. Storage units worldwide are crammed full of our extra 'stuff'. Never-ending waste and overflowing landfills are testament to our use and disposal of 'things'. Where will our rubbish live when we have stuffed all the crevices of our earth?

To consume more and more we have to work more and more, do more and more, and put ourselves under more pressure. To keep up we have to reshuffle our priorities, possibly working too much at the expense of our relationships, or losing perspective altogether about who we are and what we actually want as individuals.

How does our consumption relate to our deeper needs as human beings? We must realise that what we do unto our earth, we do unto ourselves. As long as we continue along our burnout trajectory as human beings, we will burn our earth out with us.

I watched a riveting documentary on the traditional crafting of a kimono. It took a year to make, and it was a masterpiece. Silk threads were dyed with pigments from the earth and washed in the rapids of a river. The vibrant silk was then woven by artisans with decades, sometimes over half a century, of experience in their craft. They created intricate and beautiful patterns in the fabric before painstakingly sewing it together. At last, the kimono was proudly presented to its new owner. Such craftsmanship and meaning cannot be found in large department stores nowadays, with cheaply, quickly fabricated cookie-cutter garments en masse, made from synthetic materials and dyes, sometimes by people working in unimaginable conditions.

What we eat is another piece of the puzzle. Our consumption of packaged, artificial foods causes devastating wastage, while unprocessed whole foods are far healthier and far less wasteful to enjoy. Globally, we throw out about 1.3 billion tonnes of food a year, or a third of all the food produced. Meanwhile, others on our planet go hungry. The factory farming of animals sees sentient creatures living in unthinkable conditions, subject to devastating mistreatment and cruelty. Toxic chemicals leach into our precious soils, waterways and bodies from unsustainable, fast-paced and demand-driven food production. All the while, organic farming methods are available to those honouring and protecting our earth.

The global meat production industry is responsible for more harmful emissions than all the transportation on earth, and encompasses a devastating loss of life. Studies

now suggest that a vegan diet is the single biggest way to reduce our impact on planet earth. Genetically modified crops yield cheap feed to sustain livestock for burgeoning worldwide consumption of meat, destroying vast areas of our beautiful, life-giving forests. Indeed, we have never had fewer trees on earth than we do today. Countless precious ecosystems are collapsing moment to moment, from the bleaching of our once-magnificent coral reefs to the melting of our arctic ice. Overfishing is wiping out our underwater world, with devastating forecasts suggesting oceans will soon be devoid of life. Species of wildlife are becoming sick and extinct daily, their habitats destroyed. It is all the more tragic that we have known about our earth's plight for many decades now, yet to no avail. We forge ahead.

At what point will we stop? This earth is not here for us to pillage, burn, dirty and destroy. Each movement we make to consume and degrade our earth consumes and degrades us too. We cannot live today with no thought of tomorrow. We cannot continue to act in greedy, violent and mindless ways towards our earth, animals and each other, and turn the other way. We are thinking people, and knowledge is power. Here's to us doing whatever we can, and acknowledging that our care and contribution matters. Here's to human kindness.

THE SECRET TO
HAPPINESS, YOU SEE,
IS NOT FOUND IN
SEEKING MORE,
BUT IN DEVELOPING
THE CAPACITY TO
ENJOY LESS.

Socrates

SLOWING DOWN AND FINDING PATHS BACK TO BALANCE

A sure and kind way back to balance involves mindful enjoyment of our earth and her precious resources, including our food and material choices, and careful consideration of the quality and rate of our consumption. Indeed, living with an active interest in the health of our bodies, our natural environments and all the creatures with whom we share our world is an active, revolutionary approach to greater peace on earth for all life.

How can we be kind in our daily lives, homes and communities to support the health of our earth? We can do simple things routinely, and inspire our loved ones to do the same. We can recycle, compost, ride our bikes or walk when possible. We can minimise waste by swapping disposable tea or coffee cups for a reusable cup, refusing plastic straws, using stainless steel water bottles with filtered water rather than plastic bottled water, and opting for reusable rather than plastic bags. We can choose glass or ceramic storage vessels over plastic varieties, and try reusable plastic-free wraps for food storage. We can notice the excessive packaging of goods and find earth-friendlier alternatives, such as shopping at local co-ops where packaging is 'BYO', or at a bare minimum.

We can choose simple, natural and non-toxic beauty and cleaning products for our homes, caring for our bodies, our soils and our waterways. You might like to try diluted apple cider vinegar as a cleanser, brown sugar as an exfoliant, and coconut oil as a moisturiser. For home cleaning explore bicarb soda (baking soda), white vinegar and essential oils. Being kind is so simple and rewarding!

We can donate any unwanted clothes to charity or to others we know who might enjoy them, partake in clothing swaps or market stalls with friends, or choose pre-loved garments over new ones where possible. If purchasing new clothes we can choose sustainable, natural fibres such as organic cotton, silk or linen, and ensure the clothing was produced in fair conditions.

We can keep our purchases to a minimum, mend and make do. We can pool and share resources such as tools and devices with our friends and neighbours, and meet our needs with less 'stuff'. We can choose not to upgrade our devices or possessions unless we truly need to. We do not need more 'things' on this earth – there is plenty to go around. The more we demand, the more will be supplied. Now, more than ever, we need to become conscious consumers. We are being called to live differently and more kindly. To see and enjoy what we already have, be happy with more human experiences of love and connection, and far fewer 'things'.

For daily nourishment and personal wellbeing, we can buy and support organic produce from local farmers, or grow our own fruit, vegetables and herbs if possible. We can also adopt a kind, plant-based diet. Indeed, enjoying a colourful, nourishing plant-based diet could possibly be the kindest, most revolutionary decision possible

in the face of our earth's plight. Whole-food plant-based lifestyles contribute to exponentially less loss of life on earth, less pollution, less waste, and less destruction of our natural habitat. Plant-based eating fortifies our personal health and the health of our earth.

We are seeing innovation in sustainable architecture, landscape, industrial and object design. We are witnessing the reappropriation of our waste through thoughtful recycling initiatives worldwide. The more aware we become of the significance of these innovative and earth-saving options, the more we will choose and advocate for them, from hemp and rammed-earth houses to passive solar buildings, to furniture and apparel made from recycled materials, to swimwear made from plastics retrieved from our oceans. Anywhere a garden can grow, we are seeing people yielding home-grown produce and greening our planet with their love, time and care. Seeds can be sprouted on kitchen benchtops, and fruit and vegetables grown successfully on tiny inner-city balconies. Change is beginning, and we must be an active part of it.

It is a whole paradigm shift, a holistic and fulsome movement towards kindness that we need to be a part of if we are going to change the world. We needn't feel powerless in the face of our earth's plight; our simple, daily choices matter. We must actively be the change we wish to see in our world, work collectively for the health of our planet, and help to educate and empower one another with our kindness, enthusiasm and passion. In this way we may slow down at last, love our earth, and find sure paths back to balance.

THE SMALLEST
ACT OF KINDNESS
IS WORTH
MORE THAN
THE GRANDEST
INTENTION.

Oscar Wilde

KINDNESS AND COURAGE — PAST, PRESENT AND FUTURE

Courage and kindness have preceded our arrival. Our living elders and ancestors in spirit have paved the way for us to live and see ourselves differently. This includes life-changing movements for human rights and freedom, racial and gender equality and the health of our earth. Intimate struggles in the name of liberty, acknowledgement and survival have been lived within our families and communities. An extraordinary history of pain, defeat, hope and victory has come before us. Courageous, kind and proactive people the world over, just like us, have chosen to fight for their own quality of life, and that of the future: ours.

Feeling gratitude for the toils that our forebears endured, their bravery, perseverance and vision, is not only kind – it is inspirational. While we are the beneficiaries of so much good, our revolutionary courage and kindness is still desperately needed today. In an interview with Oprah Winfrey, Maya Angelou recalled a life-changing statement she heard as a young woman: 'Your crown has been bought and paid for. All you have to do is put it on your head.'

Indeed, when we live our lives to the fullest with respect for the past, present and future, we cannot help but love, shine and be courageously kind without question. We cannot help but be grateful for our lives, and bring comfort, joy and respect to others with whom we share our world. It has never been historically viable, nor is it plausible today that there will come a moment in which the majority will vote unanimously in the name of kindness, goodness, the health of human beings and the wellness of our earth. Until the world pivots on principles of human rights, not money, this consensus will not be reached. We cannot wait for this moment to arrive. Change begins here and now, with us.

Positive change always begins with individuals making choices. It has almost always been passionate and caring minorities that have turned tides over time. Those with sheer determination, dedication, and a belief in higher love triumphing, have changed the course of history and found their voices heard.

We are thinking, feeling beings, and our compassionate awareness is power. The world changes at a higher level when we elevate our consciousness, that is, when we work individually and together towards understanding the truth, and sensing the interconnectedness of all life. Cultivating kindness is a crucial part of our personal, collective and planetary healing. The more we wake up to see things as they are, to see what is true from a place of love and hope, not ignorance, greed or fear, the more alive and healthy our today and tomorrows will become.

Our contribution to life, to our earth and to those yet to come matters more than we could ever know. When we put on the crowns that have always been ours, embodiments of our birthright, we honour our past, create our present, and shape a brighter future for those who will follow us. Our active, loving kindness towards ourselves, others and our earth day to day makes us part of the solution, rather than part of the problem.

KINDNESS AND ONENESS

Each day the world feels slightly different, and so do we. Each day the moods of the earth, the energy of her people, and the feelings felt near and far, are immense forces that touch us all.

Being human means being connected to a whole: part of something far greater than ourselves, our immediate family, friendship or work circles, or the daily worlds we have come to know. The truth of our oneness seems easy to ignore in the private, separate way most of us live today, yet our sensitivity and sense of connection with one another cannot be denied or underestimated.

Sensing our oneness brings us the deep meaning and connection for which we inherently yearn. In moments of disaster or crisis, people often come together in supportive and kind ways without judgement, fear or separation. It is a shame that facing tragedy is possibly the most obvious condition for embracing togetherness, especially knowing that we have the choice to connect in this way at any given moment. All the same, it is this triumphant, tender human spirit we witness in such moments that profoundly bolsters and affirms us.

There have been significant historical moments in which the artificiality of our separateness has been revealed. In the famous Christmas Truce of 1914, soldiers on opposing sides of World War I stopped fighting in order to exchange Christmas

gifts, share a meal and play football together. In 1982 Mother Teresa instigated a ceasefire in war-torn Beirut, rescuing a hundred abandoned and disabled children from an orphanage. For those few hours, bombing stopped over the city and was replaced by an unreal kind of calm. Little 'holes' in what appear to be hopelessly fixed systems of separateness expose our profound oneness, and encourage us to refresh our faith in life and each other.

As very sensitive people, we may experience feelings we cannot fully account for. Our lives may look good on paper, yet we may feel disconnected or unfulfilled inside. We might have all we want and need, yet sense that something is missing from our lives. We need to look beyond ourselves to the bigger picture of life, and see ourselves as part of a greater dance, moving and swaying together. It is no wonder that when our earth and fellow human beings have hurt and are hurting, we hurt too. There is nothing wrong with us, nor is it our fault. It is our humanness. Greeting our humanness with love is a necessary act of kindness towards ourselves. Being actively part of the positive transformations we seek is both healing and empowering.

Through all the seasons of our lives, kindness brings peace and joy to us in intimate and personal ways. Yet kindness is just as much the most viable catalyst for the immense, profound and positive changes we collectively wish to see on earth. We all deserve to experience a radically new, life-affirming perspective of the world as a loving place, and to readily sense our oneness with others and all life. May we all feel empowered to make a difference, be active participants in the transformations we dream of, and choose constant kindness without compromise.

I feel no need for any other faith than my faith in the kindness of human beings. I am so absorbed in the wonder of earth and the life upon it that I cannot think of heaven and angels.

☆

Pearl S. Buck

CULTIVATING KINDNESS TOWARDS THE EARTH

MINDFUL EATING

 Mindful eating is an act of kindness towards our bodies and our earth. Try gently laying your hands over your food before eating it. Thank the earth for giving of herself to nourish you.

MOON- AND STARGAZING

 Looking up at the moon and the stars is a very grounding and awe-inspiring practice. It reinvigorates the wonder and appreciation we sense for our earth. Make it a nightly ritual to acknowledge and honour our miraculous planet with your grateful attention.

SUNRISE, SUNSET

 Wake up early enough to see the sunrise, or make an effort to enjoy watching sunsets as often as possible. Observing earthly rhythms helps us to find and honour our own rhythms, bringing us greater joy and peace.

GREAT OUTDOORS

- Enjoy bushwalking, camping, ocean swimming, hiking, rock-climbing, orienteering, going on a picnic, or embracing any adventure in which you are ensconced in nature.

- Better still, spend a little time with your bare feet against the earth, a grounding, energising practice known as 'earthing'.

- Breathe fresh air, move your body in nature, and take time to enjoy the healing powers of our earth.

GET CREATIVE

- Create sculptures or functional pieces for your home from recycled items, or elements found and foraged outdoors.

- Restore old furniture with love rather than buy new pieces, or choose pre-loved clothing items and make them your own.

- Be industrious, curious and clever, and you'll not only be living sustainably, you'll be having much more fun.

SEASONAL DELIGHTS

- Choose to eat seasonal fruits and vegetables by growing them yourself, or choosing local markets for your produce.

- Connect with your local farmers, ask them questions and thank them. In doing so you'll come to connect more deeply with the food you eat, and with the generosity of our earth.

IT IS IN
NATURE THAT
REAL HEALING
BEGINS, FOR
OURSELVES
AND FOR OUR
EARTH.

m

JOURNAL PROMPTS

Ways in which I show the earth kindness include ...

Ways in which the earth shows me kindness are ...

Some beautiful things I have noticed in nature lately include ...

My favourite season is ... because ...

My favourite flowers are ...

My favourite animals are ...

My favourite fruits and vegetables include ...

Woods, beach, land, mountains, or sea? ... because ...

Aspects of nature that are worth more

of my time and attention are ...

My dreams and wishes for our earth are ...

POSITIVE AFFIRMATIONS

Kindness creates ease.

Kindness fortifies our earth.

Gratitude for nature fills me with inspiration.

When I connect with the earth I come alive.

The earth needs my care.

I sense my oneness with all life.

CONNECTING WITH
THE EARTH NOURISHES
MY SPIRIT.

—

APPRECIATING THE EARTH
FILLS ME WITH WONDER.

—

WHEN I LOVE THE EARTH,
I COME HOME TO MYSELF.

—

MY CONTRIBUTION TO THIS
EARTH MATTERS.

—

FROM LITTLE THINGS
BIG THINGS GROW.

MEDITATION

I close my eyes now,

I slow and deepen my breath.

Breathing in, I imagine my breath going deeper,

through my body and right to the very centre of the earth.

Through layers of earth, through roots and rocks,

my breath reaches the molten core of the earth.

I feel the warmth in my chest as I reach this place.

Breathing out, I exhale into clouds and stars above,

boundless and free.

I breathe deeply in and out with the earth for a few moments.

As I breathe on, the space around me expands.

I sense myself able to move freely up into the clouds,

above the clouds, up towards the sun and moon.

I float freely here above the earth.

Looking down I see the crowns of big old trees,

dolphins dancing across the ocean.

I see light kiss mountaintops,

and the luscious canopies of forests.

I float about to see all places at once.

Snowy hills to tropical islands. Sunrise to sunset.

Day and night, all at once.

I breathe in the earth's splendour,

right up and out through the crown of my head, breathing out,

back down through my body and out the soles of my feet.

In this expansive state I soar about,

breathing in wonder, and breathing out gratitude.

Breathing in I inhale endless fresh air and new life.

Breathing out I exhale old hurts of the earth and my body.

Breathing in I feel my oneness with all life.

Breathing out, I embrace the earth with love.

YOU ARE NOT
A DROP IN
THE OCEAN.
YOU ARE THE
ENTIRE OCEAN
IN A DROP.

Rumi

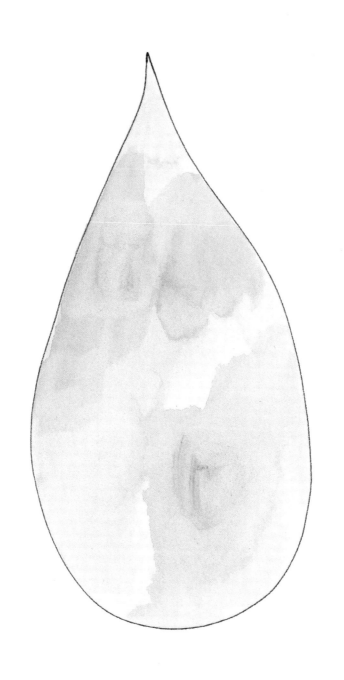

DEAREST YOU,

Cultivating kindness is a delightfully transformative and positively life-changing art. Through kindness we ease our own paths, and lighten the lives of those with whom we share our world. Whenever we choose kindness, we can feel fortified by its steady, healing magic.

Kindness acknowledges that we are in this life together: moving, learning, loving, growing and feeling together. Kindness brings us peace of heart and mind, and connects us in ever-positive, respectful ways with ourselves and each other.

Kindness involves being present with gratitude, and going the extra mile to care for ourselves, each other and our earth. It means being happy for one another in our joys, supporting and comforting one another through our challenges. It includes listening carefully, and choosing patience, respect and forgiveness for both ourselves and others.

At the end of a lifetime, accumulated kindnesses of all sorts, treasured memories of precious moments, the love we have felt for ourselves and others, the unforgettable gestures of tenderness and support we have shown and received: these are without a doubt the things that matter most.

I hope these pages may become resources for you as you walk a kinder path. May you feel more inspired, comforted and alive than ever before as you practise the art of kindness in daily life.

Meredith
♥ X

ACKNOWLEDGEMENTS

I am grateful for all the kindness in my life, and the people who have taught me so much. I thank my grandparents and parents, my brother, Nicholas, and my extended family and friends. I gratefully acknowledge the loving support of my husband, Kevin Lindemann, the kindest man I know.

I would like to thank my publisher, Pam Brewster, along with her wonderful team at Hardie Grant in Melbourne, and my lovely editor Allison Hiew. I am grateful for my book designer and dear friend Arielle Gamble, with whom I assembled these pages. Thank you to Meaghan Thomson, Mick Smith and his crew at Splitting Image for their careful handling of my original artworks. A big hug for Josette Frost, my wonderful friend and assistant.

I am thankful for Julie Gibbs, Kay Ridgway and Jeanette Barrett, inspiring women who have each helped me greatly along my path. I lovingly acknowledge my poodle, Rudi, as well, who assisted me to write this manuscript with one paw upon my keyboard at all times!

This book is dedicated to my father, Michael, with whom I talk about life.

KINDNESS RESOURCES

READ:

Kindness and Self-Care

The Art of Gratitude, Meredith Gaston
The Art of Happiness, Thich Nhat Hanh
The Art of Wellbeing, Meredith Gaston
The Biology of Belief, Bruce Lipton
Breathe Magazine
A Course in Miracles Made Easy, Allan Cohen
Destination Simple, Brooke McAlary
Happiness, Essential Mindfulness Practices,
   Thich Nhat Hanh
Ikigai: The Japanese Secret to a Long and Happy Life,
   Hector Garcia and Francesc Miralles
The Kindness Pact, Dominique Bertolucci
Love Your Body, Louise Hay
Love Yourself, Heal Your Life, Louise Hay
No Mud, No Lotus, Thich Nhat Hanh
Optimism, Dawson Church
Peace of Mind, Thich Nhat Hanh
Slow: Live Life Simply, Brooke McAlary
Soul Medicine, Dawson Church
Wellbeing Magazine
Womankind Magazine
Women's Bodies, Women's Wisdom,
   Christianne Northrup, MD
Women's Wellbeing Wisdom, Dr Libby Weaver
You Can Heal Your Life, Louise Hay
You Were Not Born to Suffer, Blake D Bauer
Your Bed Loves You, Meredith Gaston
Your Sacred Self, Dr Wayne Dyer

Connective Kindness

Answers From the Heart, Thich Nhat Hanh
The Art of Happiness, Dalai Lama
Emotional Intelligence, Daniel Goleman
The Five Love Languages, Garry D Chapman
The Honeymoon Effect, Bruce Lipton
Living Buddha, Living Christ, Thich Nhat Hanh

Real: Living a Balanced Life, Victoria Alexander
Start Something that Matters, Blake Mycoskie
When I Talk to You, Michael Leunig

Loving Our Earth

The Edible Balcony, Indira Naidoo
The Edible City, Indira Naidoo
*Grown and Gathered: Traditional Living Made
   Modern*, Matt and Lentil
Healing Our Planet, Healing Ourselves,
   Dawson Church
Mindfulness and the Natural World,
   Claire Thompson
Mindfulness in the Garden, Zachiah Murray
Peppermint Magazine
The Prayer Tree, Michael Leunig
Second Nature: A Gardener's Education,
   Michael Pollan
We Are Here: Notes for Living on Earth,
   Oliver Jeffers

Kind Eating

The Art of Wellbeing, Meredith Gaston
The Conscious Cook, Tal Ronnen
Cooking with Kindness, Pam Ahern
Crazy, Sexy You, Kris Carr
Deliciously Ella, Ella Woodward
Deliciously Ella: The Plant-Based Cookbook,
   Ella Woodward
Deliciously Ella Every Day, Ella Woodward
Feeding the Hungry Heart, Geneen Roth
Green Kitchen Stories, David Frenkiel and
   Luise Vindahl
Kenko Kitchen, Kate Kenko
Mindful Eating, Mindful Life, Thich Nhat Hanh
My New Roots, Sarah Britton
Nourishing Wisdom, Marc David
Raw, Yoko Inoue
This Cheese is Nuts, Julie Piatt
Vegan Goodness, Jessica Prescott

Kindness and Daily Inspiration

101 Moments of Joy and Inspiration, Meredith Gaston
101 Inspirations for Your Journey, Meredith Gaston
A Deep Breath of Life, Alan Cohen
*Acts of Kindness: 101 Ways to Make the World
    a Better Place*, Rhonda Sciortino
The Five Side Effects of Kindness,
    David R. Hamilton, PhD
Hay House Kindness Book
The Happiest Refugee, Anh Do
I Can See Clearly Now, Wayne Dyer
I Know Why the Caged Bird Sings, Maya Angelou
The Little Prince, Antoine de Saint Exupery
The Story of My Life, Hellen Keller

WATCH:

Bakara
Chasing Coral
The Chef's Table *Episode featuring Jeong Kwan
Consumed
The Cosmos
Cowspiracy
Fed Up
Food Choices
Food Matters
Forks Over Knives
Global Waste
Happy
Human Planet
Hungry for Change
In Defense of Food
Made in Japan (BBC Scotland)
The Minimalists
Plastic Oceans
Samsara
Seeds of Time
Sustainable
Terra
The True Cost
The War on Waste
What the Health

LISTEN:

The Good Life
Hay House World Summit
In the Company, Kylie Lewis
Louise Hay affirmations and lectures
The Mindful Kind, Rachael Kable
The Minimalists Podcast
Oprah's SuperSoul Conversations
The Rich Roll Podcast
The Slow Home Podcast, Brooke McAlary

VISIT:

www.biome.com.au
www.thedailyguru.com
www.dawsonchurch.com
www.deliciouslyella.com
www.drhyman.com
www.ecostore.com.au
www.greenkitchenstories.com
www.hayhouse.com
www.inikacosmetics.com.au
www.koala.eco
www.kriscarr.com
www.leunig.com
www.markhyman.com.au
www.meredithgaston.com
www.mindbodygreen.com
www.theminimalists.com
www.mynewroots.com
www.ofkin.com
www.tedtalks.org
www.thisnourishedlife.com
@trashisfortossers via Instagram
www.truecostthemovie.com

Mindfulness Apps:

Buddhify
Headspace
Insight Timer
The Mindfulness App
Smiling Mind

Published in 2018 by Hardie Grant Books,
an imprint of Hardie Grant Publishing

Hardie Grant Books (Melbourne)
Building 1, 658 Church Street
Richmond, Victoria 3121

Hardie Grant Books (London)
5th & 6th Floors
52–54 Southwark Street
London SE1 1UN

hardiegrantbooks.com

NATIONAL LIBRARY OF AUSTRALIA

A catalogue record for this
book is available from the
National Library of Australia

The Art of Kindness
ISBN 978 1 74379 469 2

10 9 8 7 6 5 4 3 2 1

Publisher: Pam Brewster
Managing Editor: Marg Bowman
Editor: Allison Hiew
Designer: Arielle Gamble
Production Manager: Todd Rechner

Colour reproduction by Splitting Image Colour Studio
Printed in China by Leo Paper Product. LTD